TAKE THE COMPASS

THE HUGH MacLENNAN POETRY SERIES

Editors: Allan Hepburn and Carolyn Smart

Recent titles in the series

Take the Compass

MAUREEN HYNES

McGill-Queen's University Press
Montreal & Kingston • London • Chicago

ISBN 978-0-2280-1881-0 (paper)
ISBN 978-0-2280-1961-9 (ePDF)
ISBN 978-0-2280-1962-6 (ePUB)

Legal deposit third quarter 2023
Bibliothèque nationale du Québec

Printed in Canada on acid-free paper that is 100% ancient forest free
(100% post-consumer recycled), processed chlorine free

We acknowledge the support of the Canada Council for the Arts.

Nous remercions le Conseil des arts du Canada de son soutien.

Library and Archives Canada Cataloguing in Publication

Title: Take the compass / Maureen Hynes.

Names: Hynes, Maureen, author.

Series: Hugh MacLennan poetry series.

Description: Series statement: Hugh MacLennan poetry series

Identifiers: Canadiana (print) 20230226396 | Canadiana (ebook)
2023022640X | ISBN 9780228018810 (paper) |
ISBN 9780228019626 (ePUB) | ISBN 9780228019619 (ePDF)

Classification: LCC PS8565 .Y63 T35 2023 | DDC C811/.54—dc23

This book was typeset by Marquis Interscript in 9.5/13 Sabon.

for Ruth Kazdan

CONTENTS

Contents

Contents

BEFORE NIGHTFALL

TAKE THE COMPASS,

                          take the harp, take
the FitBit and the Band-Aid box. Fold the whole
grey sheet of sky, lumpy and unalluring
into your rucksack. The song of woe, the itch,
and the predatory US dollar will follow
you without invitation. No keys or papers
needed for this journey. Pack needle and nail,
thread and wire, fragrant cathedral beeswax,
the air recently flapped under a gull's wing.
A shoe pebble to make you stop and rest and puzzle
where your other pains come from. Carry
curiosity and confusion in your hand, stroke
them with feathers and prick them with thorns
to keep them alive. Wash your face in fog,
your hands in hopefulness. No journey
is completed without yearning and a sustained
mercy for the walkers, the harpists, the injured,
the hatless, and the lost.

set out without expectation
without itinerary
as you embark on the nameless
fragmentary journey before sunset

first you feel the lift then the chill
of planetary relics departiculating
into stars and comet dust
you are moving fast now

no longer fused to the magma core
you rise   hover over enormous grey waves
sand rinsed out of your thought-gears
by the rain   the wet laundry of your emotions

flaps dry   your body lands
close to the cliff edge
arms & legs outstretched
near the ancestors' graves

the glint of a tombstone's brass turtle
is dulled by strong salt winds
your touch brightens the turtle's head
reawakens the slow helpers
the companions

you re-enter the language of high cliffs

I am in raggedy track land.
Urban Barn land. A place
with aerials and windmills
and field after field of solar panels.
Pedestrian malls and cargo
trucks pulling up to loading
docks. Solitary mothering
land. Hearts and clubs
and spades land. Diamonds, too.
Where no forest grows, where
stealthy steel and glass tiptoe in.

Yearly, the Perseids drop
with a splash like
golf balls into a pond.
Kite sky and rocky lakeshore
with a small film crew
setting up on a sandy inlet.
Herbicides leaching into the lake.
Land where warehouses
collect like cells in a neurasthenic
brain, where discarded yellow
school buses are scattered like
broken pencils. Where Ajax with his
magnificent shield was conquered
by his own sorrow.

become our spirit guides
Can they cross back
into the calamities of our world
to nudge us into action
open-heartedness   persistence
Or must they assume another form
avian   oceanic   oaken
riverine or stone

Can they swim back to us
through the newly discovered
Ice Age channel beneath Montreal
to warn us that our comforts
will be shredded
our homes flooded or burned
our soil salted and dreams dissolved
if we don't speak out
for the air   the oceans
the planet's creatures
the miracles beyond

ENTER THE EYE

                    sky window
the size of a small lake
in the library's roof   unblinded

& blinking at nimbus clouds
that presage rain   snow
grey hints of release

where mercy & pleasure
& discovery flow in
my simpleminded wish for

every city   every neighbourhood
to have a library with
an oculus like this

where children's questions
may rise unbidden
into the stratosphere

                            in the moment
before dusk falls into our hemisphere.
His silver flute summons my cymbals –
we make a great clash that opens
into laughter. The joining ripples
the way orange lilies spread throughout
my untended garden, a tubular under-
ground grasping. That rough scent. Weed-ish,
but with a ragged beauty. A clamour that takes
the nervous right out of me.

                          These are the helpers –
invisible, but we can hear and feel them.
Like last night when our young neighbour
sang "White Rabbit" on her porch and Grace Slick's
spirit helicoptered over our street, lowered
the trembling rabbit in a woven grass
basket among us. No watch in his pocket.
No pocket. Apparitions. We trusted
what we heard more than what we saw.
We washed our hands to Gloria Gaynor's
survival song – she kept us in tune all
through the night. I dreamed I bought
an electric guitar, pink, star-shaped.

Well, we're all kind of blue now.
Blue poured over the entire
world, like that long-ago image
above a storefront in Chengdu –
I didn't understand the Chinese
characters, but the tipped can
pouring its viscous liquid over the globe,
thickest at the North Pole, streaming
over Siberia, slipping past the equator,
over Lima, New Delhi, Cape Town –
fluid fingers of paint grabbing
the world from above. Now

every time I hear the virus's name,
I see it printed in 48-point
sky-blue Helvetica on
a blank page, a neighbour's
front door, my bar of soap. But,
Miles, thank you for those long
tender trumpet notes carrying
our sadness, climbing it up into
smoothness, that particular kind
of everywhere sans serif sorrow.

a fire escape
of any colour to lower into
the southern hemisphere,
a rescue, a lawn of vibrant fescue
and an indoor shovel in case snow
piles higher than her doorframe.
A lifeline caesura or the blessed
pause from calamity, a thermos
from the now-defunct
Scarborough Thermos factory
to keep her tea warm within
its beautiful silvered-glass flask.
Roses, always roses, even
January roses – their thin scent.
Embroideries or paintings
or b&w photos of roses would do,
the pearly-grey shading of a petal's blush.
Oh, and that particular soar
in a song from Mercedes or Dinah or KD.
New boots, a pair for the wearer
who dislikes either a winter-wet
right foot or a soaker in her left.
Stability, instability, a new
position on the fulcrum.

BELLA CIAO

As directed in the workshop, I drew my "voice flower"
which looked like those spiky pink blossoms on a dollar
                                                store cactus.
Later I whisper-sang along with others my determined wish

for a revolution *now. Beautiful day, hello, beautiful
                                        person, hello!*
My voice rounded and lifted and sprang
forward when I came to the word *now.* But now

the sun is setting, it's banding yellow-pink across the city's
horizon. Yes, I understand life's a rough ascent,
an icy path, sometimes a precipice to hang from.

I apprehend the perils and paralysis. Still, the melody's
sweet ferocity filtered through my shaky whisper-singing,
to reveal the layers, layers like pages in an illuminated

book, each page a long and colourful story-song.
That determination! Now the clouds are pulling apart
in strings like spun sugar – how granules turn into lengths,

given heat, given velocity, given spin. Is there a star to name,
a sunrise to welcome, a person to greet? I want to sing
to end cruelty – *Bella ciao, bella ciao, bella ciao ciao ciao!*
I could use my cactus-flowering voice.

ALL CLEAR

Stamped down but not-yet-
sullied snow on February streets –
startled & heartened by the small
magnolia tree's comma-shaped
buds, thick at the head & tapering
at the tail, their grey plumpness.
A nod of thanks to these promises.

On Chester Avenue a winter bake sale
held by four or six or eight children, signs
lettered in pink & blue & posted in snowbanks –
Bake Sale to Save Australian Animals.
My heart lurched & warmed & failed –
I did not stop, wanting to get
to class on time, even though
the young girl with the very brown
eyes looked right into mine, asking
me to buy a cookie or a bun. How
could I have turned away?

Fresh road snow, roof & lawn snow, sidewalk
snow, snow rows along the curbs – all
gleaming with the slight grey etchings
of last night's full Aquarian moon.
The snowfall has not covered any thought
of the burned Australian animals, but
four or six or eight children are clambering
all over it, melting it away.

COURTHOUSE SQUARE PARK

For three seasons it's warm & quiet enough
to get a good night's sleep in this tiny park   alee
to the noisome downtown winds

Very little light at night from the surround
of office towers   The park enclosed
on the south by the quiet burble of three

rectangular & uninscribed fountains
Off to the east trellises form an overhead
corridor of espaliered roses & clematis

The back of two fancy restaurants to the west
& from the north the stately old limestone
courthouse now another restaurant

jail cells still in its basement   *how quaint*
the bars & locks & cast iron peepholes
In the small park's centre a marble sculpture

of seven enormous books   beautifully askew
on a large plinth   The plinth it's been said
marks the former site of public hangings

its plaque at a distance   to prevent
the haunt of treasonous rebels who failed
to defeat the unelected powerful

THE DAZZLE TIME

The skies are emptying of airplanes, but
filling with drones. My mind is crammed
with intentions that take off but never land –
they hover mid-air at the grey horizon, shadowing
the late afternoon sun.

What strange internalized days
we are thrust into – some welcoming
them, most chafing against their blankness.
David Milne, married twice but a solitary man,
painted city streets, lakes, and leafy trees

pressed fanshape-flat against the sky,
often a woman sewing or reading
in a wicker chair, a still life with a cobalt blue
medicine bottle. *Whatever's in front of me.*
Developed the practice of leaving a blank

space somewhere in the canvas, called it
"the dazzle area." One unpainted
building, say, in a crowded cityscape, to
snatch and release your attention,
engage it elsewhere on the canvas.

Blank – before it meant white, it meant
to shine, to flash, to burn. Is this
the blank spot in our years?
Can we polish our inner lives
in isolation, brighten our songs and odes?

But now it's time for more
window-gazing. The number of kids
in the tiny park behind our house: zero.

and hello, pincushion! Hiya, seam guide
& zipper foot. Hello, straight pins
& little wire tension spring. Hey,
old pinking shears – now your toothy
bite is duller than your squeak.
Ah, foot pedal, you are a large
black mouse at my right foot

(am I also right-footed?) & warmest
greetings to my spools of many hues
& now absolutely essential needle threader.
Oh, little lozenge-shaped light bulb, you still
illuminate! Thanks for your endurance.
After a twelve-year absence, I return –
but O my machine, have you gained weight?
You must be nearly thirty kilos! Still,

old friend, you're another instrument
I can sit down at, say *Buongiorno* & start
creating. Please remember to call me
a *sewist,* our new gender-neutral
title. A destructive matchmaker
has stitched us back together, but
while sirens roar across the firmament,
your thuddety-thud-thud makes
such soothing tracks.

VISTA GRILL

"[Life] :... sits a fisherman
down beside you at the counter who says, Last night
the channel was full of starfish."

Eleanor Lerman, "Starfish"

I'd like to sit at that counter, listen
to a fisherman's news of a channel
full of starfish. I'd like to enter,
for my first time, the 24-hour diner
around the corner, the one where
short-order cooks serve

midnight burgers for every kind of hunger.
The diner that never needed a lock,
but when the pandemic closed in
the owners had to install one.
A handwritten note on the glass door –
6 eggs, a loaf of bread & a bag of potatoes

for the first 75 people on Saturday
morning. *Make your own breakfast*
and think of us, read the sign.
My partner said, *Getting rid of*
inventory. The starfish around here
could be the white-streaked scilla

spreading through periwinkles
on people's lawns every spring.
Or daffodils – that brightness.
Maybe the blue jays landing
on a branch of our lilac so it springs
up & down for a couple of seconds.

Our starfish could be the potatoes
in the paper bags. And maybe
the owners and cooks are fishers,
heading back out to deep waters.

the iceless morning, its pervasive
greyness: concrete sky over infected
water. After the walk and the singing
that was both alarm and homage
to the river's buried meanders, buried
but still swelling up into a baseball field,
we climbed the hill to the broad street.
Cars weren't stopping though I pressed
the crosswalk button five times.

My friend and I were talking about
the foxes my cousin had seen
in that ravine, and the coyote
I'd glimpsed. We finally crossed,
stepped up onto the curb, where we found
a red swastika painted on the sidewalk
and up the yellow fire hydrant.
Walked past, trying to blur that image
with the river's rushing greyness.

ALL CLEAR

It comes out in March, by the back fence ...
Lorine Niedecker, "Progression"

In July, yes, & June & May & even all
those months before, say, back to March –
each drew silver & plastic & elastic songs
out of our tightened lungs. The sewing machine
repaired, the masks colourful & haphazard.
Finally, May Day, the doctor called with results
& questions about poetry. His shyness
both infected & cured me. It turned into
something stone-hard that I could lob
from the city's highest bridge clear into
the unvaccinated river. But no, but no,
that's unkind – the doctor was considerate
& knew exactly where my fear was sitting.
Front row centre.

SUCH THINGS THEY PLANT
AROUND MY HEAD

consumed in flame or set atop
a wind-grey mountain outcrop

wrapped in grasses & a white cloth
lightly visited by the pepper moth

or in a rock-sealed passage mound
what will surround my head?

under the garden's paperbark maple
we discussed the elders' dark

stifled deaths in large lonely numbers
tiny air sacs fluid-filled & jumbled

trenches for potters' graves   unclaimed
names marker-scrawled on pine lids

FORGIVENESS

In my hair I carry the seed blossoms
of several Norway maples – each moment
beneath their ample shade a rainfall
of futurity and chance. How plentiful
their tiny yellow blossoms, how thickly
they carpet the flagstone walks, umbrellas,
tables, chairs – an overabundant
year, say the city arborists.

I don't want to malign any tree
but almost daily I mourn the magnolia
that sickened and died, its roots
girdled, its light and air stolen, its soil
poisoned by the leaf fall of the three
Norway maples who command
our tiny front yard. I keep trying
to forgive their invasiveness, forgive

the city for planting so many of them,
but forgiveness is useless, for me
and for them. I will never harden
my body or stretch my limbs
far into the sky, never hold
a goldfinch in the crook of my elbow
or reach my fingers deeply into the earth
for residues of groundwater.

STONE PENCIL

SUMMER ICE

There was an icebox in the kitchen of the Lake Simcoe
cottage that my parents rented for three summers.
Down the road was a deep-dark barn, which I remember
as circular and without doors: both unlikely. Cracks
and gaps between the barnboards let me peer inside at
the ice blocks harvested from the lake in winter. They
were covered with sawdust and stacked like giant steps to
various heights. The spaces between the boards bothered
me. *How come the ice doesn't melt with all this summer
heat pouring in*, I asked the adults, each of whom gave
answers I couldn't fathom.

It is a very hard job to cut and store and deliver ice,
my mother told me. My uncle, an obstetrician, paid his
way through medical school delivering summer ice.
Those thick black tongs and the frozen weight, how he had
to hoist each ice block over his shoulder onto his back,
enter kitchen after kitchen, to place it in the top half of
an icebox. My mother the eldest, he the youngest sibling.
A slight blond man with five daughters. A joker who
loved the horses. Didn't take my mother's cancer as
seriously as I thought he should. But he was right – she
recovered fully. Decades later, after her funeral, he said,
She raised me. They both fell through the ice into the chill
inky lake of dementia. Neither could be lifted out with
ropes or love or tongs.

STONE PENCIL

"Do you remember learning to spell?"

Brenda Hillman,
"As the Roots Prepare for Literature"

A first year of school in France, no finger painting
or blocks or sandboxes, just plunged
right into cursive & make no mistakes. Somewhere

is the photo of me in that dark Alsatian classroom –
holding my slate & a stone pencil, thin as a tulip stem,
for scratching French words onto its surface, later to be

wiped off with a damp rag. That impermanence: seven years
postwar, but paper still rationed. In the photo, I see my left
margin widening with each line, a handwriting habit I still have.

Tested on my first day back in Canada, sent to the front
of the room, the teacher's long pointer thrust into my hand –
I knew what to do. Walked my way across the alphabet,

tapping each card with its lowercase & capital letters
above the blackboard, giving each its English name,
pronouncing its sound. The alphabet old hat to me,

the other children just starting. Show-off.
Tall for my five years & jammed into a Grade One class
of 48 children, thanks to the 1950s baby boom.

Finished my recitation, all those blank stares dissolving
my confidence. Suddenly self-conscious, the pointer
a withered tulip, as if under a spell.

ELEMENTARY

It is time to begin the alphabet, specifically
the Greek one, whose first two letters
name the whole mighty string of symbols
that we give to four-year-olds –

an endless thread placed in their hands
like the one for numbers. But with this September's
turbulence begins the renaming of hurricanes
and tropical cyclones. We used to call them

after saints' feast days – such a large
supply. Then we turned to Anglo names,
Brenda and Charles and Doris, stopping this year
at Wilfred, like my uncle the doctor. We "retired"

the names of storms that had swallowed
uncountable lives and homes and shorelines –
Hazel, Katrina, Sandy. It's early now in cyclone
season to have used up this year's list

of hurricane names, so we are starting again
with Alpha, Beta, Gamma. Will twenty-four letters
be enough to spell out this year's loss, death,
hubris? Still so many lessons churning, unlearned.

little square
bottle   the same
age as me

little square
label   pencil-
thin brown line

of dried perfume
within   just lift
the cut-glass

stopper   release
my mother's lost
fragrance

in the Fifties
no one cared
about Coco's Nazi

lovers   with the war over
wealth was what people
wanted   or at least

signs of it   some
elegance   on the bedroom
dresser   something

small that said   Paris
glamour   a scent that would
last   for decades

the unconscious likes to hide its intentions
surplus motives & credit cards   its file
of inventions & evasions

in the studio I noticed   but did not remark
upon the grey torso   a dress form so essential
to the proper fitting of a garment   how lovely

her arms were   how smooth her hands
as if sculpted   I see the new father crouching
on the floor   beside him a photo

of his newborn   I recall the photo of me in France
standing in the open door of a train
about to depart the Gare du Nord

I look happy but my father on the platform
is in tears to see me leave   it is 1985
I am 37 years old   there is no young man

about to fire a gun   no one who's
grabbed me from behind
& is about to choke me

what is the fabric of the veil
behind which the unconscious
hides   is it a net curtain

with hundreds of sequins   or steel mesh
or plant-based like a lavender sachet
O those tiny purple buds on every stem

what I love most in the garden
is to grip a stalk of rosemary
at its base & gently pull my hand up

over its pointy tips   walk around with
my hand covering my nose & mouth until
the scent fades   the loss of a child

in a school shooting never fades
I stand at the studio window   watch
a young woman in a red parka   the handle

of a huge purse over her arm   she walks
alone into a night   that will be a minute
or two shorter than last night

SONNET BEGINNING WITH A LINE
FROM CARSON'S TRANSLATION OF SAPPHO

they let their wings down

she let the kings drown

I let my parents down

(I did not keep the faith)

we turned the sound down

the down on their wings was silent

they put down their arms (the war was over)

the war is never over

our hopes were overblown

they unfurled their wings and flew

like the arms of an old nightgown

blowing on a clothesline

now grimy rancid snow has turned to ice

and oh we do not want to fall down

UNCOUNTABLES

When the young woman asked me, "How much?"
I answered, "Four." The young woman, a brighter
version of myself but still uncertain around the edges,
wanted to know how much sugar, how much rope,
how much tenderness, how much money and music

and time. How much war. I was surprised
she thought to call on her older self, and why it is only
now that her question is reaching me. And of course
how to answer her. She is asking about uncountable
things, and I am answering her with a single number.

A number for evenness, harmony, solidity, balance –
the number of children in our family, the number
of seasons and compass points and legs on a chair, as if
that will satisfy her. A kind of blindness in the question,
a kind of blindness in the answer. And yet. And yet.

MEDUSA'S HAIR

After that incident
in Athena's temple where
Poseidon dishonoured Medusa
Athena ordered Medusa killed

not Poseidon

But really the young Medusa
fled & survived   She bleached
her dark snaking hair anime white
tied it back in a scrunchie
Her beauty shone with laser-like force
over many centuries & still
endures

though her holographic gaze-power
of turning men to stone rarely
petrifies

seems she must collect a stone   a ribbon
a coin   a basket   a bus ticket or a bracelet
from each country she visits   each lover she's had

a rough stone   for scratching out   grim months
a smooth millefiori glass weight   for tossing
into a star-reflecting lake   on an August night

a basket   the smaller the better   as the willow
or raffia or roots dry & crackle   seems she needs
to press her fingers against   some other woman's

handiwork   imagine her skill   her life
can she pawn the jewellery   hammered silver
slender wire   broken clasp

she needs the coins & tickets for her return
but what colour   what fabric for the ribbon –
is it silk or twine or rope   for rescue or ascent

TO WARD OFF ADVERSITY

THE INVISIBLES

After Brenda Hillman, "Poem for a National Seashore: ix,"
*"In spring when the field starts to think & the invisibles
are relaxed…"*

yes, invisibles here too in spring
when our city backyard furrows
its several thin brows & the park
behind it with the wading pool
wonders what is scratching
at it from below   root-thinking
worm-crawling   or what pokes
& tickles it from above   remembers
when geese arrived each spring   waded
& traveled on   but today
it hums for the scilla bulbs
& their deep blue thoughts
it warns us of the secret military
march of ants   into the crumb-
abundance of our kitchen

Perhaps it was a giant leaf – mullein,
say, or sweet coltsfoot – impermanent
and doubling as a fan. Followed the mask
made of a small mammal's skin,
a black outline inked around the eyeholes
like the circles around a vireo's eye.
Then a strip of bark, two torn slits
for eyes. A piece of wood,
carved, sanded, ochre-painted.
Blue feathers glued in rays
around a papier-mâché face. For

protection or ritual. Or at Samhain,
a disguise, a ruse, a jesting flirt.
Or the bandit's need to dissemble.
Now the ceremony is broadly public,
required, gauzed and elasticized.
We bare our eyes but cover the mouth
and nostrils to keep us from breathing
in a lung-destroying flake,
to keep us from spray-speaking poison
in the shape of tiny beaded crowns.

THE JUGGLER

Yesterday a great many pellets
of graupel shot out of the low grey sky –
bouncing ice-balls!
Spring's thunderous shout muffled
by its cloudy facemask.
We have been too knotted
into death counts & pollen counts
& approval ratings to hear
the red-winged blackbird's *what-about-meeeeee*
at the edge of the train tracks.

Today was brim-full of intentions, then
emptied out by midafternoon. Tomorrow
will haul in its own disappointments
& spill them onto our doorstep
like a torn mesh bag of birdseed or
another skyful of ice-pills. But tonight
we'll have lentils & loaves & a few
new ideas but mostly messages
to answer. I will think about mandalas
& Scarlatti & why the twenty-one women
cloaked together in Varo's surreal grey garment
thrill & scare me all at once.

POROUS

an unmarked calendar tacked high onto
the tamarack's trunk   clouds leaking danger

but Mars darns with a red cedar needle
and a single green strand   pinpricks

through our daily fabric   ask what traces
the mineral lode   who spins the naked rigour

of the ICU roulette   beds empty and fill
reveal the squander   o to find an anchor

in the charcoal clamour   snow rests
under the cloudless sky   days drain

through the holes in my kitchen colander

HELLEBORES

Spring mizzle dampens day's end
All the sun can do is scratch an orange
crayon line across the horizon
Not wild enough for me   I complain aloud
but I carry this drizzling sunset   into my sleep
to douse the avid monstering fears
that travel incognito   Overhead they extend
their talons   locust-swarm against
our windows   then drop five-petaled flowers
that turn into cougar footprints

Hellebore stems & leaves are poisonous
but its dried rhizomes were once prescribed
to cure madness   Lenten roses   charming
old name   Blossoms facing earthwards
reluctant to open   show their sex
speak their cream satin glamour   folding
in upon themselves just as we do

pull out your art supplies   the garden's
about to pop   the forsythia's preparing
to open its million four-fingered hands
and yes there will be raking   but first
you need to slow your mind to present tense
you also need a soft HB pencil & any old paper
your green & yellow pencil crayons   maybe a fine-
tipped black ink pen   to record this ebullient
growth   before you hack it all back
in some desperate pruning fit   your perfectly
self-sufficient friend is writing you about
the perverse friendship of death   another
is weeping her way towards it wordlessly
sans glamour   sans memory   sans sang-froid
you can find so little to say to them
but to ward off adversity   silence will not
do   instead forsythia & phone calls
& your clumsy little drawings

has been declared
the Colour of the Year, and the city's scilla
are all over it. Rather, they're all over the city,
beautifully speckling Rosedale Valley Road, where
tiny blue blossoms cover the roadside's northern slope,
almost opposite the cemetery where my friend
is buried.

Some call these flowers invasive,
but they spread a Classic Blue shield against
anguish and fear. A colour, says Pantone,
to bring reassurance, confidence, connection.
Every spring the scilla re-enter, and finally,
this spring a dozen are creeping
into our front yard. I've never seen these
perennials

in a nursery but a lovely
budding belt grows on Davenport Road,
shoreline of the ancient glacial
Lake Iroquois. I am planning a late spring
larceny under nightcover with a trowel
and a plastic bag – to root them
into our lives.

ODE TO THE EMERALD ASH BORER

Your elegant jewel casing belies
lethal scribbles, the poisonous
galleries that mark your industry –

but if I could collect you and a dozen
of your kin, I would braid you
into a thick iridescent band

that I could slide onto my ring finger,
the finger whose *vena amoris* flows directly
to my heart. I'd wear you as an enamelled

adornment like those fashioned by Victorian
jewellers – diamond brooches in the form
of swallows to bring loved ones safely home

or filigreed pendants shaped like dragonflies
for tender beginnings. Your delicate presence
on my hand would tell of your voracious

destruction of beauty and equally,
the beauty of destruction.

DEAR AUTUMN MANDALA

                              yellow leaves surround
your red chrysanthemum core   I have spread garden-

gathered fragments on newspaper obituaries
thinking   *this will do*   as surface   as backdrop

each iris blade in your nine points   a pencil of grief
pointing outward   zig-zag sharpness piercing me

dear spiky image   your scent has long speared off
into evanescence   but you brush the softness of white

elderflowers against my inner wrist
daily your Japanese maple leaves curl up   arthritic

fingers   each finger could cut new red lines
into the palm of my hand   in your centre

leaf-sorrows weighted down   by three grey stones
smoothed in the loudness of Lake Huron waves

the mighty lake   that soothed us   amidst the deaths
its shoreline etched with conquest and carousels   I long

to walk again at sunset beside its thundering
roar   my footprints a trail across its shoreline sand

tell me a little joke   jagged green strokes
bring me the hermit thrush   sweeten

the reluctance out of me   spill lily seeds
into our television reports   break

the bad news into nine living petals

think of leaving
your baby in a forest
like the woman   in that war

half-teaspoon-sized water
droplets   on the surface
of sharp-edged

birch leaves   dipping
in & out of light   think
of babies or newly

unfurling shoots
spiralling their way
out of the soil or

a significant branch into
air   foliage high &
thick   sweet birdness

encircling the moment
she walked away

FOR YOUR HEAD

                    make a halo, a wreath, a circlet
of bright green aspen leaves. Crown your dismal
           thoughts & unruly feelings with a tiara.
Find small red things, a cranberry or rosehip or yew berry
           to trim your sorrow-filled week, to be the eyes
that your eyes can't see out of. With grass dew,
           paste a rose petal on your forehead, and smear
a lick of honey on each earlobe to sweeten
              whatever you hear. Breathe in jasmine
to intensify your memories. Pick four small leaves –
           one for Hope, one for Trust, one for Rage,
the last for Desire. Lay each briefly on your tongue,
           just taste, don't swallow. Open your mouth,
let their power beam into the world's countless
           troubled and troubling zones.

Luckily I have a lot of highbrow
knickknacks. A hurdy-gurdy
& a shipshape buzzsaw. Quicksilver
shoeshine & flim-flam pyjamas,
all kinda loosey-goosey.
Tick-tocks for the stock pot.
A crackerjack and flip-flops
that go clip-clop if you jazz up
the soles with some klunky
razzmatazz doodads. Streams & streams
of sticky tickertape picked up off the wet
streetscape after a rainy parade
to celebrate the wicked war's end, or
after the snowstorm when the dream team
was elected, but ding-dong, now
they're dead. A bright whirly jukebox
that plays a lot of artsy-fartsy claptrap,
but one treasure is the old cassette
of Brendan Behan singing
Jingle jangle goes the ould triangle –
his party piece, and mine.
A chock-a-block collection that just
looks higgledy-piggledy but melts
the hearts of the hoity-toity & tickles
the toes of the whippersnappers
& the pipsqueaks. What good fortune.

MY BEDSIDE TABLE

KLETIC AT THE BLOOD WOLF MOON

o my love   when you awoke
sickened & flannel-voiced   snow
had sifted heavily into our sleep
meringued the cars & fenceposts
(o goddesses of serenity & euphony
what are your names that I might
beseech you)   booted & down-
vested I strode out to clear
a luminous high-banked pathway
to wintry wellbeing   tears
freezing to my cheeks
tonight my love   earth's
shadow will swallow the moon
& your calamitous cough

Asclepius, god of healing and medicine
has lent us his wand or maybe his walking stick
          entwined with a snake
as sign for honourable treatment & recovery.
          Are the snake's eyes open?
Asclepius welcomed the ill and injured
          into his temple where serpents
slithered on the floor among them.
          While patients slept, Asclepius poured
the names and dosages of remedies
          into their dreams.

But what is the emblem for sleep?
          Perhaps a musical instrument laid on its side
a drum leaning against a wall or my uncle's
          penny whistle resting on a chair
with a leather cord twined around it.
          The cord an emblem of the banished snake
and the banished language   the suppressed song.
          Each morning we shed our dreams
as a snake sloughs off its skin   as we hope
          to shed our maladies and despondencies.

DREAM LEXICON

Dreaming of periwinkles signifies a lack of song in your life.
A dream of brushes or worms is a message to attend
to the small or prickly. Tinfoil and thunder in the same
dream recall the ordinary drama of your mother's life.
Moth-eaten holes in all your sweaters at precisely
the same spot on the cuffs urge you towards a tenuous
opening. The recurring dream of glaciers is of course
nostalgia for former lovers. A dream of maps provides
interesting but unreliable clues to past and future travels.
It's odd we so rarely dream of beds, but arranging
pillows or cushions is a form of confession, uncovering
sins. A message of trauma and loss from a dream
of saunas and moss. However, abundant green lingers
from the tamarack dream, assuages longing and guilt.

no hotel room   instead the foot
of a benevolent volcano
which steamed & wept & sighed
one of a chain   a guard row
that ran the length
of two continents   a barrier
against oceanic flooding

no flowers   just dark
grey sand   chunks of lava
dulled & hardened   we slept
at the volcano's base
listening for the earth core's
whimpers   feeling the fitful
twitch of its muscles

no birds   clouds & stars
swirled above us
the open-air swoop of bats
& the dance of gnats
in ascending & descending
spirals   the soundless labour
of tiny creatures

but there was a slow river
a channel of hushed thought
flowing between us & the red core
our river joining what flowed
deep & molten beneath
it was night   it was almost love
it was almost strong

stitch a woolen sonnet that scratches
your neck   reddens your head
you'll want to pull it off
though it's meant to put you to sleep
me to sleep   us to sleep
him her them zem   really it's an ear-
flap sonnet   a doormat lyric
a car door wooden floor empiric-
al pillow   stuffed with bristly wool
spun from uncountable insomniac
sheep   spin spin spin   you can wear it
on an airplane   pull it down over
your eyes & ears for a joyful trouble-
free flight

    what keeps you awake?

MELA

she tells me
get some Mela-
tonin at London
Drugs 16 different
brands & dosages on
the shelves empty sold-
out spots among them she
needs Extended Release 10 mg

there's an epidemic of sleeplessness
in our small neighbourhood our
neighbours' brains & their
underactive pineal glands
blue & green screenlight
tricking their mentality
awake a lot of SAD-
ness afflicting us

mela from the Greek for
dark or black   for our daily
calamities an industry gleans
the chemical bed of crystals over
which flows the inky river of night-
sleep   a machine powders its sand into
10 mg capsules   counts them into gleam-
ing white plastic bottles   & seals them shut

There was danger in the sleep lab. Already full of danger with more peril seeping in. The wail of sirens poured through the window into the fifth-storey room. The room was lit with fluorescent hydrangeas – thickly petaled microphones picking up the murmurs and rustles and whimpers the sleeper made. The sleep lab was not a hotel room though it was aiming for that ambience. Aiming and failing, on account of the high single bed and the fluorescence and the wires and the lack of a minibar. She was in a near state of undress except for the 30 electrodes pasted to her skull, throat, chest, arms, legs with collodion glue, the glue whose fumes felt like tentacles. The multicoloured wires were similar to embroidery threads in their profusion and tendency to knot. A silken tube carried words from room to room. The softest of pneumatiques if you please. But immaterial, untextured, wisp-ish. There were encephalographs taken and words tested into the pale green sepals at the base of the knowing microphone. The sleeper would never find out if she spoke or what she said. Then there was the recording of her dreams that the technicians kept for themselves. The crooked vinyl blind rattled in its metal track and finally one side completely derailed. She could peer through the gap to see footprints imprints bootsteps trampled all over the city street's snow, a surface now similar to the grey hatched moon. She was as skittish as a deer. It was early, it was late, it was not yet dawn.

MY BEDSIDE TABLE

I keep a silver pillbox of ampersands
in the drawer & on sleepless
nights I pop a few to reconnect

me to my dreams & to counter-
act the question marks
I swallowed all day

ampersands are smooth
& curlicued & much more genteel
than the plus sign

they have been a bit lonely   feeling
disrespected   ever since they were
lopped off the end of the alphabet

they are glad to be of service
in reuniting us with our wishes
unbidden fantasies   dead

relatives & even our worst
horrors which we can
though shaken   wake up from

I take the professional grade
they are pliable & elastic
they can be chewed so their effect

is stretched out for a whole night
of oddities & uninterrupted
yearnings & surprising reunions

The burial of memory and those innocent outstretched
       palms. We learned that gesture in childhood,
along with the shrug. *It's only two hundred years old,*
       said the sociologist about our economic system.

And his point? Its fragility? Its resilience or endurance,
       like the titanium implants in so many elderly
joints, or its viral adaptability? Perhaps its in/stability,
       like a kayak crossing the Hecate Strait?

An economics as changeable as the moon, our nightly
       guardian who also wanes & disappears.
But now with plans to colonize her, conscript her
       as a launching pad to the universe, her cries

will do no good, her metals will be mined, also her salt
       and silicon. Ten swords plunged into her back.
What threat to her, to us, to the politician
       on the podium? There's that shrug again.

WAVE-WASHED

NOT MY IDEA

                    The singing
wasn't my idea but I did it to reach you.
I interrupted the old statues, cloaked
in gilt-hemmed robes & speaking
all at once, a cacophony of dead
languages. The saints were hatless but haloed,
crowned with an energy that radiated
heavenwards, through the roof
of the magnificent new library
where you can borrow laptops by the hour.
They had followed me there in search
of a new kind of church
                         but all I wanted
was a typewriter without its ribbon
to cut the letters of words into a stencil,
to roll out a hundred copies of the famine
song for you on the mimeograph machine,
the one sung all through the eras before
any saint was born. On the passerelle
the wind said, "Scatter," and I knew
that's how you'd hear my song.

BUS TICKET & WINDOW SEAT

I am the pages of the household
calendar & you are the colourful
images above the grid of days.
Oh, that relentless flap of months –
even so we are grateful for the flapping,
wish it to continue effortlessly.

I am half-remembered lyrics
& you the well-rehearsed melody,
but our harmony definitely
soars. You are the city rabbit
that visits our garden, but rarely,
& I am the wooden fence she slips through.

You are the red-tailed hawk
perched on the bank's coat-of-arms
& I am not prey, but rather
admirer on the pavement,
looking up & taking your photo
against the blue sky. Who is turtle

& who gull? Lemon tarte & whole
grain bread? Microphone, megaphone.
Starfish & hot pink glove lost
on a city street. Bus ticket & window seat.
Atlas & road map, whirling pages
of every island & ocean in the world.

if you take the largest
chunk of lapis lazuli
you can fit into
your hands   and hold it
for many minutes   at least
until the stone warms
and your hands cool
your spirit will enter
a dominion   a stratosphere
or maybe just a landmass
of urgent beauty   a rocky
terrain of sky and a sunlit
lake of the bluest water
bluer than cobalt or
International Klein Blue
the colour's temperature
will heal your injuries
it will pitch you towards
an impenetrable twilight   as if
through a deep synoptic
array

FLORIOGRAPHY

You have sent me Blackthorn
and a stem-knotted bouquet
of my favourite spring flower,
the Chequered Fritillary,
emblem of persecution. Delivered

a hanging pot of my beloved
Lobelia, whose message
is malevolence, and you have
surrounded us all with Lavender
for distrust. You want

from me a Peach Blossom
to signify *I am your captive,*
and another sign of surrender
with a single persimmon –
Bury me amid nature's beauties.

With Borage for bluntness,
I send back Basil for hatred.
To fortify my message,
I tie together Wild Licorice
with Belvedere, both crying

I declare against you,
I declare against you,

For myself, I call the florist
(she is still working – delivery only)
for a beribboned nosegay
of Lily of the Valley,
like those sold on Paris streets

for Mother's Day to mark
the fragrant return of happiness.
And though it's out of season,
a spray of Mistletoe,
which murmurs *I surmount difficulties*.

For us all, Snowdrops and a few
Coreopsis for everlasting
cheerfulness. Oats? asks the florist,
surprised. Yes, I say, include a spray
to bring us *the witching soul of music*.

HOW MUCH OUR BODIES

have in common
with tree bark   turtle shells   rocky
stone paths   parched landscapes   even

moonscapes   these weathered envelopes
that contain our beings
& permit the passage of microscopic

organisms   across   through
into a cracked floor
where a virus can bide

see how a tiny cart has etched two
even ruts   across a red desert
a pathway   pocked with holes

but what is the cargo

let us unpack the wet tent   badly folded
& stored away for the winter
spread it flat   with the crosshatched

palms of our hands   or count
the fissures deep in an ocean bed
for an octopus to slither into

hair-stalks jutting from crannies
up close   the skin's roughness
comforts me   swellings

flakes   abrasions & folds
tenderness travelling
over   outward   deep within

hold her naked   skin to skin
the best soothing treatment
for a newborn in distress

or an adult

STILLNESS, FLOATING

What ocean floats the hand-
knotted brown-string net
beneath the crystalline mummy

the mummy whose brain flashes green-green-red
whose heart is a plastic peristaltic pump
throbbing on a blood-red blotch

whose kidneys call back and forth to each other
in dandelion whispers & mouse chatter
What weighs down the figure

on her bed of blue salt   nylon
filaments tethered to long tusk-coloured
rosary beads   The netted centrepiece

of a modern pyramid
is she semi-alive   semi-dead
on the calm saltwater of a cove

a water-logged crypt   a flooded graveyard
Throw me a kapok lifebuoy to rescue her   toss me
my rubber bib overalls   chemical resistant

& waterproof   my poncho & blue goggles
my salt-stained polka-dot plastic boots
Hold hard my lifeline as I set out

I'll shout the fifty abandoned & banned
names for cyclones to rouse and revive her
to catastrophize the silence out of us

How to display for public
memory the strikers' defiant footsteps, their songs
and chants, the overhead helicopters, the fears
of those kettled into an intersection, tear-
gassed and baton-beaten?

In room after room, hang
banners, spread placards and photographs
at eye level within a hundred glass cases.
Lay open the enormous post-contact books, superbly
scribed and illuminated, the colonial laws and exclusions,
punishments and executions.

Suspend the frayed and bloody
bullet-holed shirt in its own tall glass case.
Is it enough, the small placard with the wearer's
name and the April 1916 date? (How brown
the blood after a century.)

Make note of the resistance,
the readiness to say *no*. Sit on the park bench beside
the nameless bronze figures chatting with each other.
With your back to the Stonewall pub, warm their hands,
ask how long it took

to smile again after the police.

SOLSTICE, LATE AFTERNOON

is this what my death will feel like
I asked myself   as I lay coughing
into the darkness   the rasping stronger
each night   climbing a rickety
ratcheting ladder up   or down

into who-knows-where   I keep all these
fears lidded in a small red enamel
pot   one of a pair I bought
in the Friendship Store in Chengdu
or maybe in Shanghai   in the other I keep

my hopes   good wishes from friends
& three tiny tokens of my partner's love
Bernadette says   *women love later*
in a more complicated way   also tiny
are the juniper needles I brought

inside today & put on the window-
sill   their berries white-
dusted and bone-hard
from the studio window I watch shoppers
pour up & down the market streets

the sun at its most distant point
but not yet set

WAVE-WASHED

Clouds tear into long shreds across the horizon,
and gold-pink-red striations begin to glow
over the old pre-glacial lake – the lake where
we had a week of sunsets except for the night
the greyness poured in. A tangible
hue that I could reach my whole right arm into –
it held the veiled future and the dim past,
into which I could thrust my erratic
unknowing left arm and still hold in both
my hands the biggest losses, the sweetest
vows, the fearful look on my mother's face
as she was going into surgery, the swaddled
firmness of an infant's body. Then in the
brightness of the present you found my hands,
placed into them shells and smooth wave-
washed stones and a gleaming chestnut – hard
shiny elements to pacify a furious future.

BE PLANETARY,

the poet advises –
live without horizons, acclimatize
to a new light cycle (dawn or
dusk may take eons to arrive).
Accept what she calls the violence
of sunsets, a violence she admires.
What do planets do that we could
emulate?

Of course the circling,
an orbital reverence for the sun,
roiling in the dark spinning bath
with asteroids and our planet
cousins, ringed or ringless,
rocky or gassy, metallically
colourful.

But also a loneliness
the planets don't seem to mind,
perhaps even prefer. Would we
retain all our senses but touch?
It seems a fearless self-sufficiency,
a distance from companions that
would frighten me, but she calls it
the calmness of your spirit.
I will work on this.

"enter the eye"   This poem honours Calgary's Central
Library, opened to the public in 2011.

"what she needs"   A response to Ronna Bloom's poem,
"clearing out the shelves,": "What does she actually
need? / A toaster? A teapot? A pen?" in *The More*
(St John's, NL: Pedlar Press, 2017).

"Bella Ciao"   The song, "Bella Ciao," originated in
nineteenth-century Northern Italy as a song of women rice
field workers declaring determination to end their oppression.
It was adapted by anti-Fascist partisans during World War II.
The cactus referred to here is the pink Gymnocalycium cactus
flower, a "top indoor ornamental plant."

"Vista Grill"   After Eleanor Lerman's poem, "Starfish,"
in *Our Post Soviet History Unfolds* (Louisville, KY:
Sarabande Books, 2005).

"after the river, remembering"   A poem inspired by the
line, "Hateful words survive in sticky clumps," by C.D.
Wright, in *One With Others [a little book of her days]*
(Port Townsend, WA: Copper Canyon Press, 2011).
This poem is for Dilys Leman.

"all clear"   After Lorine Niedecker's "Progression," *Lorine
Niedecker: Collected Works,* ed. Jenny Penberthy (Berkeley
& Los Angeles: University of California Press, 2002).

"Such things they plant around my head"   The title is
borrowed from Lorine Niedecker's Spanish Civil War poem,

"1937," *Lorine Niedecker: Collected Works,* ed. Jenny Penberthy (Berkeley & Los Angeles: University of California Press, 2002).

"Forgiveness"   "The Norway maple is allelopathic. Its roots exude a toxic substance that kills things that grow underneath it, allowing for the tree to continue growing ... its leaves contain a toxic latex that harms insects and pollinators ..." The Weather Network, https://www.theweathernetwork.com/ca/news/article/highly-invasive-tree-putting-canadas-iconic-sugar-maple-at-risk#:~:text=The%20Norway%20maple%20is%20allelopathic,the%20tree%20to%20continue%20growing.

"Summer Ice"   After Ann Carson's "Mercy is from a lake," in "Uncle Falling," *Float* (Toronto: McClelland and Stewart, 2016).

"Stone Pencil"   After Brenda Hillman's question, "Do you remember learning to spell?" in "As the Roots Prepare for Literature," *Seasonal Works with Letters on Fire* (Middletown, CT: Wesleyan Poetry Series, 2015).

"Elementary"   The first line is borrowed from Robin Blaser's "The Hunger of Sound," in *The Holy Forest* (Oakland, CA: University of California Press, 2008).

"Midwinter Day"   After Bernadette Mayer's *Midwinter Day* (New York: New Directions Publishing Corp., 1982).

"Sonnet beginning with a line from Carson's translation of Sappho"   From Anne Carson's "Fragment 42," in *If not, Winter: Fragments of Sappho* (Toronto, ON: Penguin Random House Canada, Toronto, 2002).

"the invisibles"   After Brenda Hillman's poem "Poems for a National Seashore: ix," in *Extra Hidden Life, among the Days* (Middletown, CT: Wesleyan Poetry Series, 2018).

"To ward off adversity"   The title and "the perverse friendship of death" are borrowed from Etel Adnan, *Time,* trans. Sarah Riggs (New York: Nightboat Books, 2019).

"The Juggler"   The art referred to here is *The Juggler* (1956) by surrealist artist Remedios Varo (1908–1963), https://www.gallerywendinorris.com/news-reviews/varo-moma-acquisition-announcement.

"Ode to the Emerald Ash Borer"   In response to Mark Dion's "The Life of a Dead Tree" exhibit at the Museum of Contemporary Art, Toronto, May–July 2019.

"Quivering toward light"   The title is borrowed from Lorine Niedecker's Spanish Civil War poem, "Wartime," in *Lorine Niedecker: Collected Works,* ed. Jenny Penberthy (Berkeley & Los Angeles: University of California Press, 2002).

"Everything's Hunky-Dory"   After Harryette Mullin's "Jingle-Jangle," in *Sleeping with the Dictionary* (Berkeley: University of California Press, 2002).

"Kletic at the Blood Wolf Full Moon"   Kletic: an invocatory poem, one that calls upon a deity or other force.

"my bedside table"   After Eve Joseph's "The poet keeps a jar of commas …," in *Quarrels* (Vancouver, BC: Anvil Press, 2018).

"Ten of Swords"   Websites such as https://www.popsci.com/elements-mine-on-the-moon identify some metals and elements on the moon of interest to mining companies: silicon, rare earths, titanium, aluminum, water, precious metals, helium 3.

"Floriography"   Wikipedia defines floriography as "a means of cryptological communication through the use or arrangement of flowers. Meaning has been attributed to flowers for thousands of years, and some form of floriography has been practiced in traditional cultures throughout Europe, Asia, and Africa ... Interest in floriography soared in Victorian England and in the United States during the 19th century. Gifts of blooms, plants, and specific floral arrangements were used to send a coded message to the recipient, allowing the sender to express feelings which could not be spoken aloud in Victorian society ...," https://en.wikipedia.org/wiki/Language_of_flowers.

"how much our bodies"   This poem was commissioned for Jess Holtz's exhibit, *Skin,* featuring electron photographs of skin printed on fabric, with poetry embroidered onto her photographic images (https://www.frogheart.ca/?tag=jess-holtz).

"Stillness, floating"   This poem was written for the opening of Elaine Whittaker's installation, "Murky Bodies," Redhead Gallery, Toronto, February 2020.

"Solstice, late afternoon" After Bernadette Mayer, Excerpt from MIDWINTER DAY, copyright ©1982 by Bernadette Mayer. Reprinted by permission of New Directions Publishing Corp.

"Be planetary,"   After Etel Adnan's collection, *Shifting the Silence* (New York: Nightboat Books, 2020).

ACKNOWLEDGMENTS

Thanks to the editors of the following anthologies and online or print journals for publishing these poems:

Arc: "All Clear."

Best Canadian Poetry 2021, ed. Souvankham Thammavongsa (Windsor, ON: Biblioasis Press: 2021): "All Clear."

Event: "Forgiveness" and "Wave-Washed."

The Goose: "Everything's Hunky-Dory," and "My Bedside Table."

Ice Floe Press: "After the river, remembering," "Enter the Eye," "outskirts," *https://icefloepress.net/2020/04/08/two-toronto-poets-a-three-day-series-part-1-three-poems-by-maureen-hynes/.*

Juniper: "Newborn" and "Take the Compass."

La Presa: "Fitful."

The League of Canadian Poets' "Poetry Pause" on the League's website, 13 March 2022: "Bus Ticket and Window Seat."

The League of Canadian Poets' *Poem in Your Pocket* booklet and postcard project for National Poetry Month, 2022: "For your head."

Literary Review of Canada: "Floriography for the Pandemic."

The Litter I See project (https://thelitteriseeproject.com/) by Carin Makuz: "mela."

The New Quarterly: "Where we slept that darkest night."

The Quarantine Review: "The Dazzle Time" and "Kind of Blue."

Queen's Quarterly: "On Chester Avenue."

We are One: Poems from the Pandemic, ed. George Melnyk (Calgary, AB: Bayeux Arts, 2021): "The First Mask."

Especially deep bows of thanks to the following people
for their generous support and-editing, their encouragement
and inspiration:

First and always, Ruth Kazdan, for love and music
and the daily delight of such good cheer, and for holding
the compass;

Ronna Bloom, for kindness and laughter and insight;

John Reibetanz, for leadership and wisdom, and generous,
warm-hearted editing;

Jim Johnstone, for sharp-eyed editing and support;

Hoa Nguyen, for brilliance and encouragement,
and for creating a huge poetry community;

Arleen Paré, for friendship and laughter across
the continent, and for shared discoveries;

Ruth Roach Pierson, for our years of friendship, travel,
film, and poetry companionship;

Jane Springer, my first editor (in 1980!) and generous
friend, and who still offers to read and help me with
my writing.

As a longtime member of the following writing and poetry-
focused groups, I have benefited enormously from the
friendship, encouragement, and brilliance of:

All the women in The Electronic Garret, with special
thanks to the brilliant instigator, Tanis MacDonald.

The Grenadier Group: Pramila Aggarwal, Ann Irwin, and Jean Unda.

The Inconvenients: Kelley Aitken, nancy viva davis halifax, Anita Lahey, Dilys Leman, Sue MacLeod, and Sheila Stewart.

The Miss Vickies: Linda Briskin, Jennifer Rudder, Liz Ukrainetz, and Barb Young.

My poetry reading group of deep readers: Steven Carter, Sue Chenette, and Jaclyn Piudik.

The Victoria University group: Alan Ackerman, Allan Briesmaster, Sue Chenette, Richard Greene, Carla Hartsfield, Marvyne Jennoff, Robert Johnson, K.D. Miller, Mary Nyquist, Chris Pannell, John Reibetanz, Leif Vaage, and Laura Zacharin.

Sunday morning workshops with Barry Dempster, Jim Nason, and Maureen Scott Harris.